For Jenny Lumet

Grudge 🐾

For Jessica Schmidt

Robb Pearlman

General Editor: Ben Robinson
Development Manager: Jo Bourne
Author: Robb Pearlman
Artist: Walter Newton
Designer: Katy Everett, with thanks to James King and John Ainsworth
Sub-editor: Alice Peebles
Production Manager: Siobhan Hennessey

With thanks to the team at CBS: John Van Citters, Marian Cordry and Risa Kessler

Published by Hero Collector Books, a division of Eaglemoss Ltd. 2021
Eaglemoss Ltd., Premier Place, 2 & A Half Devonshire Square, EC2M 4UJ, LONDON, UK
Eaglemoss France, 144 Avenue Charles de Gaulle, 92200 NEUILLY-SUR-SEINE

ISBN 978-1-80126-047-3

Printed in China

10 9 8 7 6 5 4 3 2 1

PR7EN012BK

www.herocollector.com

STAR TREK

DISCOVERY
THE BOOK OF
GRUDGE

as told by
ROBB PEARLMAN

Introduction

I can't tell you how many questions I get. If it's not "Please, My Queen, do you prefer to be addressed as 'Your Highness' or 'Your Majesty?'," it's "Why are you waking me up in the middle of the night?" or even "I'm deathly allergic to cats – where's sickbay?" But perhaps the question I'm most often asked is "When are you going to write a book?" I'm sure this universal need for my unique perspective is catalogued in any number of sphere data or Starfleet archives, or buried within any number of Soong or Coppelius-android's internal systems. So, if for no other reason than to be left alone, I present my first book.

You're welcome.

I think this will give you an idea of just what I think about everything, and what you should think of me. I've also allowed myself to indulge in some poetry, proof that I've some artistic muscles to flex beneath this magnificent fur. As I am unwilling to speak directly to anyone, the publisher insisted I work with a writer who holds me in high regard and is committed to telling my side of every story. He was expected to work around my eating and sleeping schedules and did so, without complaining. At least I didn't hear any complaints, as he often spoke to me, for some idiosyncratic reason, wearing an oxygen mask. I'm big enough to indulge other peoples' eccentricities, as long as they treat my own with the respect and deference they deserve.

So, I hope you enjoy my book and give it more starred reviews than there are stars in the Alpha Quadrant. And if you don't, just remember that I have direct access to all of Starfleet's communications systems and can easily alert every feline on Earth to the fact that you've disrespected their queen.

Grudge 🐾

I'd very much like to thank Grudge for the opportunity to work with her on her book, and for committing to a paws-on collaboration by sitting on me while I convalesced from my deathly cat allergy in sickbay.

Robb Pearlman

"I have been,
and always will be,
your Queen!"

Time

Depending on what planet you're on, what sun you're passing, or what temporal anomaly you find yourself in, I've learned that time is nothing but an artificial construct. So it's in everyone's best interest to synchronize everyone's clocks to me.

Grudge on . . .

Space

I do not like space. It's too cold, and everything in it is so far away from each other that it's impossible to find a cozy corner, box, or nook to squeeze into.

Grudge on . . .

Mycelial Space

Contrary to its name, there are no mice in mycelial space.

0 stars.

"Today is a good day to leave me alone."

Grudge on . . .

Black Holes

More light escapes from a black hole than interest
I have in talking about black holes.

Grudge on . . .

Verukin Nebula

Ground Zero for The Burn, which I've been told is a terrible thing that happened. But I'm much more interested in the Cat's Eye Nebula, which I'm sure was named in my honor.

Haiku

I am awake now

So you must be awake now

Your Prime Directive

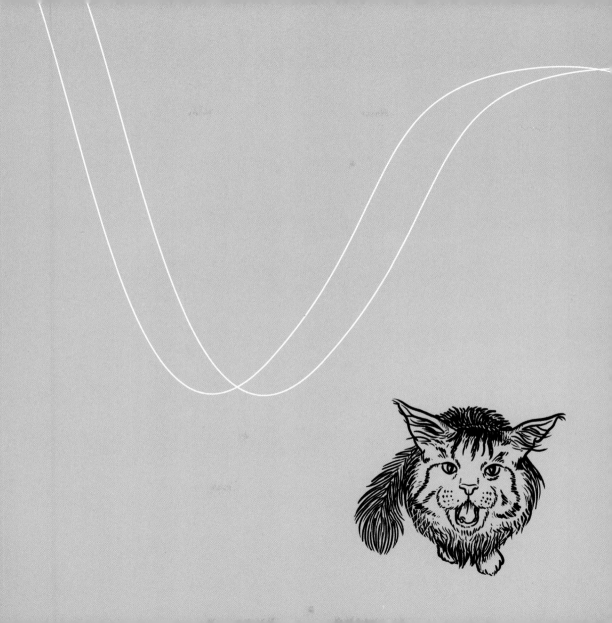

Grudge on . . .

The Burn

The Burn was a cataclysmic, universally devastating event that fundamentally changed the very existences of a myriad of species, planets, and organizations 125 years ago. Millions of beings died, and economies and social structures were left in tatters.

Can we get back to talking about me, now?

Grudge on . . .

Humans

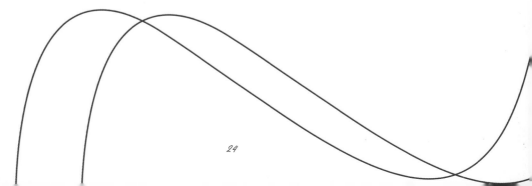

Humans were domesticated by cats millennia ago, so we have, for the most part, a very symbiotic relationship. Humans provide cats with food, toys, and a fresh litterbox. Cats, in turn, provide humans with a reason to live.

Grudge on . . .

Andorians

Unlike Earthlings, who will make you move if you lay on their faces, an Andorian's already blue in the face. So you'll need to listen for when they start gasping for air. Then, since they're awake anyway, make them give you a snack.

"Meow it so."

Orions

Though I have to admire the way some Orions scheme about and use others for their own purposes, fundamentally they're Andorians, but without the fun headgear. Which means they're of even less use.

Grudge on . . .

Size

Whether your size is the result of genetics, a thyroid condition, or from loving the taste of tuna, I hope you love your body as much as I love mine.

United Federation of Planets

Unlike the multiple worlds and species that have united to ensure my safety and comfort, the United Federation of Planets is dedicated to working together for everyone's benefit. Which I guess is nice, too.

Haiku

Ensign Tilly's hair

Andorian antenna

Best toys on the bridge

Grudge on . . .

Starfleet

As far as exploratory and defense services go, it's fine. But you'd think, after all this time, they would have found the time to give me a rank? What's above Admiral?

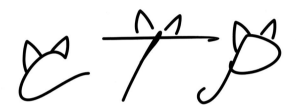

I very much appreciate that Starfleet has instituted the Cat Training Program to teach their crew how to behave like me. Seeing them run through the hallways as if chasing a mouse, watching them gain the confidence to tell others what to do leads me to believe that they're learning by my example.

Haiku

Transporter problems

Starships and shuttles all crash

I land on my feet

Universal Translators

There are countless languages spoken in the universe, so it's best to just remain silent and have the humanoids try to figure out what it is you want. And even if they guess it on the first try, make them keep guessing. It builds their self-esteem.

"Khaaaaannn't you just feed me?"

Grudge on . . .

Cleveland Booker

My human, Cleveland, is the best kind of human to have. Not only does he treat me like the queen I am, but he also makes sure everybody else knows to do the same. I'm glad I chose Book to be my human.

Grudge on . . .

My Ship

Enjoying small spaces is my thing. So, I'm glad Book provided me the opportunity to sit in a box in a room, on a scout ship that's docked in a room on another starship, that's docked in Federation Headquarters, located within a distortion field.

"There's catnip in that nebula."

Discovery

The only advantage to going from a scout ship with a crew of one (two, if you insist on including Burnham) to a *Crossfield*-class starship with a crew of over 100 is that there are so many more beings to do things for you.

The Crew of Discovery

It's important to pay attention to see when the crew thinks the ship is in trouble. Because when the chips are down, the crew will spring into action and save the day. And it's while they're saving the day that it's easiest to hop onto the table and eat the chips they've set down. I like mine with a little salt and mayo.

Warp Drive

If a warp drive is going to let you get me more Kwejian catnip quicker than we would at impulse speed, then let's fly!

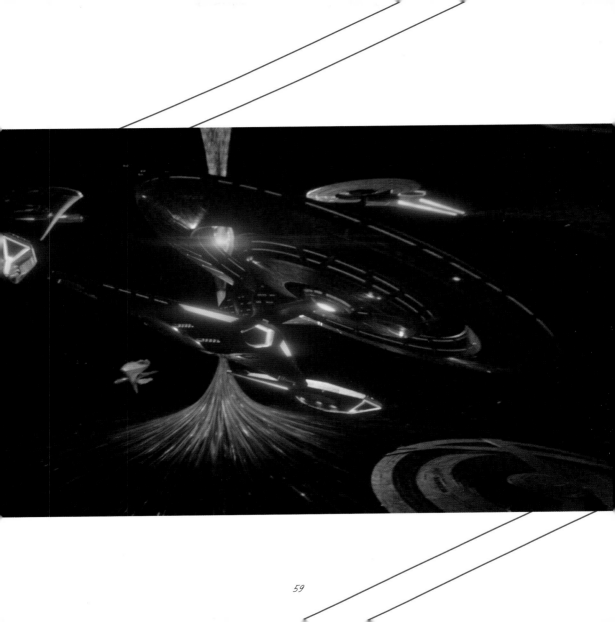

"I am not energized."

Grudge on . . .

Dilithium

Luckily, these are not the same crystals that keep my litterbox smelling fresh, so neither they, nor The Burn, have any meaning for me.

Grudge on . . .

Data Sphere

No matter how all-knowing a sentient, super powerful being claims to be, it will never know the exact right moments to start and stop petting me.

Sickbay

I get that Dr. Hugh Culber basically came back from the dead, was instrumental in keeping the *Discovery*'s traumatized crew working as a cohesive unit, and helped solve the mystery of The Burn, but Dr. Tracy Pollard made my foot feel better so she's my favorite.

Michael Burnham

I was a little annoyed when Book invited Michael to live on my ship, but she seems to make him happy, so I allowed it.

And when he's happy I'm happy. Mostly because I get extra treats when he's happy. Which makes me happy.

Haiku

The darkness of space

The blazing light of a sun

Romulan catnip

Grudge on . . .

Adira

I have no problem with this kid talking to their invisible boyfriend, Gray, all the time. But once they start trying to talk to me, we'll have a problem.

Grudge on . . .

Sylvia Tilly

I give credit where it's due, and (though I will deny admitting it) it is certainly due to Ensign Tilly. As I am not a people cat, I respect her admitting – up front – that she wasn't a cat person. In addition, I very much appreciate the fact that she thought I was diabolical enough to eat Michael Burnham.

"My needs outweigh the needs of the many.

Or the few.

Or anyone."

Grudge on . . .

Phillipa Georgiou

Only another queen can truly understand how heavy the weight of your crown is. So as a matter of professional courtesy, we've silently agreed to stay out of each other's way.

Paul Stamets

& Jett Reno

They're both brilliant engineers and prefer to work alone, but she always has snacks. I like her more.

Grudge on . . .

Saru

For some reason, Saru does not sense impending death when he's near me. That's on me. I need to try harder.

"It's possible to commit no errors yet still lose. That is not a weakness. That is life with a cat."

Grudge on . . .

Dogs

Ugh.

End Transmission.

Grudge on . . .

Spot

I don't know her.

Grudge on . . .

Instincts

Always go with your instincts.

And my instincts are telling me that I'm done.

Haiku

Pet me the wrong way

And you will wish you were in

An agony booth

Robb Pearlman

Robb Pearlman is a pop culturalist and a #1 _New York Times_ bestselling author of more than 35 books for grown-ups and kids, including 5 _STAR TREK_ books: _Fun with Kirk and Spock, Search for Spock, Body by Starfleet, The Wit and Wisdom of STAR TREK_, and _Redshirt's Little Book of Doom_. He is also a publishing professional who has edited a host of pop culture and entertainment books including _Bob Ross's Happy Little Night Before Christmas, The Bob's Burgers Burger Book, Stuck on STAR TREK, The Princess Bride: A Celebration_, and the memoirs and monographs of award-winning animators Don Bluth, Bill Plympton, and Ralph Bakshi. A sought-after guest and host at pop culture conventions and events, Robb is a recurring featured crewmember on the official _STAR TREK_ Cruise and was an on-air commentator on _National Geographic_'s "Generation X" docuseries.

Walter Newton

Walter Newton was born in 1981 in Glasgow. He remained there for the next 21 years, attending the Glasgow School of Art before being lured to the bright lights of London and the Royal College of Art. After fifteen years of living in England he returned to Scotland, where he emerges from lochs and stands on top of misty hills, with his whisky-soaked kilt and ginger locks flowing in the wind, as well as drawing pictures and sporadically animating for anyone that will let him near them.

"Cat'plah!!!!"